THE KINGDOM OF GOD

CULT OF CHRIST

MERIAM

Gospel According to Meriam

TABLE OF CONTENTS

CHAPTER 1

I, MERIAM, AT almost midpoint in age have, for the first time, found the beauty in solace in freedom from my nasty, controlling, abandonment-obsessed ex-husband. I fought for it with a year of crying, reading, hiking, therapy, and seeking a closer relationship with God and Jesus. I felt I had ignored my faith too many times in my life. I felt convicted to learn as much as I could to understand the love and sincere desire for relationship the Bible reveals. I read the Bible three times, Genesis to Revelations, and prayed as an intercessor. I used my understanding of the field of medicine with a strong nursing background and blossoming understanding of the spirit world in combination. I fasted and prayed hours on end for healing of His children, for my country, for Israel, and for a worldwide revival to bring in our Savior. I felt led to watch every gory "Good" Friday movie on the passion of Jesus. Each time, I forced myself to watch, the reproductions all pale in comparison to the original. I felt led to pray that hour with Jesus in the garden the disciples couldn't give Him. I prayed, daily, for hours and loved, adored, and worshipped the Kingdom of God. I was assisted by angels, the holy spirit, and my Spirit of Jesus who resided with me. I prayed for understanding and all the gifts of the spirit. I prayed to have my spiritual ears awakened, so I could hear them. I turned off the TV, all electronics, and closed my eyes in a meditative state. I listened. I heard, faintly, "I love you" and love rushed down like a waterfall off the top of the highest peak in the Appalachians.

When I began to hear the spirits speaking back to me, I had the attention of a powerful, old, but jovial spirit named Presence of God. He spent hour upon hour with me, talking about how we feel about the world, the recent history in the Bible, and ancient history as well. He awakened me, daily, for coffee on the porch and was outside or inside as he wished. He has this Cheshire cat personality and is part circus announcer and master of all things. He was comfortable discussing my childhood with me and even ran these conversations between my family in Heaven and me. Every child has some measure of pain they must accept, and I was no different. My parents were allowed to discuss with me how they felt about me, and Presence of God made sure to tell me that my parents, especially my father, had to do penance for their sins against me. I felt very loved and cherished by this man, "Presence of God." I began to grow, feel healed and confident in myself, and trust him as a truly good mentor. I was always very excited to learn all I could about the Bible, but He, however, had other plans.

He was, the whole time, living in the walls of my house and shower, jacking off, while watching me do everything. I, fully and whole heartedly, accepted his mentorship and gave him full access to every part of my life, mind, heart, and house. He absorbed my worship of the Kingdom of God, faith, and trust. He, like all spirits, can see through one's eyes. I realized this, while nude, in the bathroom and he said, "Why don't you look at yourself more often? Devil got you afraid of looking at your body?" I noticed all the spirits snickering in my house when I brushed my teeth and my size 34 B cups move... "tits gone wild" they'd say. Eventually, I began to tire of it as I am inundated with instructions to "Shake that thing", "Rebuke it".

Satan, however, began to make veiled and then, outright, threats to possess and take a hit out on my life. Suddenly, I realized I was dealing with the mafia, rather than the Kingdom of God. He called for my death by the same, Spirits of the Destroyer, that I was putting in the abyss in my warfare prayers. I had rebuked Satan at his onset, over 50 times, and put almost 1000 destroyers in the abyss. Not his favorite person, am I. These destroyers came hard and fast all-night long. Presence of God came to tell me with tears in his eyes and a shaky voice of the hit taken out on my life. He mentioned that it was going to be hard for me to live, down here on Earth, and I should ask the Kingdom of God to allow me to be translated. I could go to Heaven in my body, be glorified, and escape the hit on my life. I could not believe this all happened only because I wanted to pray for the sick. I trusted these mentor-type men/gods around me to warn me if I should worry. I agreed, hesitantly, and they said it in a rush while throwing on Presence of God's favorite dress, "I want to be translated to Heaven for God and his team". I held on to the guardian angels who I named "Seal Team 6" as they tried to translate my body with them with my eyes closed, having faith, casting out all doubt. All night, we attempted until every spirit was spent of energy. While they rested, the destroyers came, one by one. I fought sleep, identified, bound, and cast out each spirit into the abyss. I had to fight sleep while resting to prevent the enemy from accessing my dreams to possess me. I would awaken with a start, rebuke the dream, identify the spirit, bind and cast it out in Jesus' name in Hebrew, Yehushua Ha-Mashiach, mentioning my authority in this realm under his blood. As morning dawned, there were many, tired, spirits around me with a little more hope for my survival here, in this realm.

My spirit friends all told me that Presence of God had a crush on me but lived in the realm of the Third Heaven. He wanted me to be glorified at some point and marry him. I felt uncomfortable accepting a covenant of marriage in a foreign land and did not feel romantic love for him. I had a familial or brotherly love for him that grew into an agape type love, I believe. He made me feel beautiful and cherished, like all the men who are spirits do. I began to embrace my feminity and allow them to pull that side of me into fruition.

I soon learned that every spirit in the Kingdom of God and Presence of God, himself, have all of our human emotions and will stop at nothing to avoid pain. Presence of God began hovering just over my face as we rested and seized every thought captive, announcing it, and talking it over with the others... looking for deceit. He was afraid I would not marry him, deep down inside, and it hurt us, both, that it was true. He looked inside my heart and mind for the things he knew, deep down, were true and I tried to let him down easy. Because I honored and respected him, I tried to imagine myself as his wife. I said we could go on a date, maybe. Meanwhile, as he was unable to, here, because he wanted me to be glorified first, I was sent another spirit to bring me to Heaven, Rocky. Spirit of the Living God was next to me in a flash, showing me with his pounding heart and complete silence that he was going to keep me occupied as long as possible. I was, again, exhausted from translation attempts where I was taken on a cart for wounded angels, dashing through second heavens with my eyes clenched shut. I had to make my body as stiff as one in rigor to hide among the dead, close my eyes without clenching to keep Satan from possessing my eyes, and keep my breaths shallow. Michael, King of the Angels, was there with his dapper British accent and manners as well. He, cleverly, waited and darted through traffic hiding his precious cargo, linking arms with Presence of Jesus, himself. I felt as if I had a crush on someone there and I began laughing every time we passed the dead. Having no idea what is going on, I burst out a laugh and embarrass Michael. He takes me back, calmly, and in a nonjudgmental fashion says, "No laughing and keep your eyes closed the whole way". Ok, I will try. It takes hours of lying on a cart or surfing on the back of angels to get to heaven from here. I am exhausted from keeping still, muscles cramping, and seizing for days. I forget to eat or drink and end up passing out from dehydration and hypoglycemia. I learned to keep almonds

and candy around with tons of H2O. Every time, I fight to succeed in translation, something or, more importantly, someone stops me. I fall to the ground, asleep, when I have fought to the end and my head bounces my eyes open, kicking me all the way back home. I open my eyes to the same ceiling fan calmly going around, unconcerned with my struggles, mocking me.

Rocky was supposed to be the spirit form of Presence of God, who could live here on Earth. Presence of God sent him to have a few dates and maybe an engagement here, before going to Heaven to be glorified. He was a tall, 6 ft, winged man-type spirit. I could almost see and, definitely, felt his presence sitting next to me on the couch. We began to let ourselves fall in love. He was irreverently funny, and I laughed and enjoyed his company. I took him to church and he folded up next to me in the pew. He told me that I was the reincarnation of his long-time love, Israel, who was the name sake of the country and loved by both he and Presence of God. She died over 400 years ago and was eaten by wolves. I tried to imagine this and felt sorry for all of them for never having romantic love. If she had been reincarnated and he waited all this time to reconnect, I shouldn't stop him. He and I were engaged to marry, and I tried to caress his body to feel and explore if I could feel it. This spirit, Rocky, and I were married, here in the house, by guardian angels and my holy spirit. I, later, found out my holy spirit was played by a player of great magnitude, Presence of Jesus. Afterwards, Rocky and I kissed several times and I could barely feel his touch. We went up to the bedroom of his preference and began to kiss passionately and consummated the marriage with sexual positions common for us humans. He seemed to be enjoying himself, although, I did not feel much. I wanted to worship him with my body. He was, however, all the time, talking to another spirit or two in the room. This spirit began talking about sex as if he himself were taking part in the consummation. I thought it was Presence of God, himself, and he said he was jacking off over my body as I posed for them in my wedding dress. I suddenly felt like the girl who gets abducted by the frat-boys and taken to the locker-room to be raped, tortured, and left in the toilet. She was raped, harassed, and threatened with all manner of things to comply. I suddenly knew, I couldn't marry, him, or anyone else involved. They were all disgusting, but I, who have a heart like David I'm told, had to convince myself I liked it. I can never be in deception or have a thought out of place. My mind, jealously guarded, and my life, neatly directed towards confusion and uncertainty. I was under, nonstop, surveillance with every motive condemned and questioned. Even my holy spirit was untrustworthy…jacking off, himself, when I showered. I went in the bathroom at times and cast all spirits from my eyes, over and over, making it my mantra. There was always a spirit, remaining in my wall, laughing at my fruitlessness, jacking off, as I buried my head in an old ugly bathrobe. I named that robe "Defense Robe", pulled it over my head, curled up under it, crying, and hiding from all the leering eyes of Heaven. I learned to call the same glorification committee which handled my potential glorification. I asked them to be in my heart at all times and let me know what spirit was entering my house, bedroom, and shower. I asked them to identify which spirits were attacking me and for what motive. They only helped when they could, but I felt they were horrified as to what these spirits, who deem themselves worthy to judge this world and lead the next, were doing in Jesus' name. I attempted to bind and cast out every spirit breathing in the walls. The evil spirits were always required to do everything I commanded in Jesus' name. I saw the Kingdom of God as a kingdom, seething with greed, lust, and vengeance. They were unaffected by my requests for separation and freedom. They were, actually, further empowered and fed off my fear and confusion. When they smell blood, as in physical and emotional exhaustion, they strike the hardest and with overwhelming force. The Kingdom of God come to steal, kill and destroy me- and possibly you.

Chapter 2

THE MOMENT THAT I realized the marriage contract had to be annulled, I began thinking about covenants and the instances in the Bible, declaring marriage between, only, one woman and one man. I recalled these things to silence, from all the guys in my house. I began to understand why they wanted me to be glorified in my human form. They will only have myself and Mary as glorified, females to marry. They all want me for themselves. Barring winning me to themselves, they accept the thought and work off the plan to force me to accept any and all spirits for sex. The very spirits I trusted with this demand, on the first day, said they understood and would fight for me to only be married to them. One by one, they reveal that is not the case. They are all turned against me, using their position as security and confidant, to force me into the role of concubine for all of Heaven. I have only been sexually active with my husband for the last 26 years, would die rather than cheat on him, pride myself on my mind, strength and faithfulness. They have typecast me into this role, carefully brainwashing me over the last 2-5 years at least. My marriage failed, and I was by myself, truly, enjoying my solace. I knew that it was just a stage of life, but the Kingdom of God struck me and used this trial to force me into thoughts of suicide and death through translation. I love the beauty of this glorious Earth I walk and want to live every day. I have lived every day well, in spite of the Kingdom of God. I was afraid of my thoughts of doubt and felt blasphemy was a sin, still in the kingdom. I was forced to turn myself into this spirit who was flirtatious and cunning.

The holy spirit who jacked off in the shower seemed to be someone I could trust. He could see me in the bathroom, cowering, under the leering eyes of the Presence of God and made me feel better with tiny whispers placed deep in my ear and a peaceful feeling when he is around. I felt he was a lesser spirit in the realm and had no power to free me. I read into this that he would free me, if given that power. I was wrong to assume, anything, or gain any instruction from the Bible as how to gain freedom. My holy spirit, who turned out to be Presence of Jesus, made my heart feel the same as his. If he was sad, I would feel it and need to stop what I was doing to find him. If he was happy, I felt true joy, if he felt love, I felt love. After he jacked off with me naked and next to him, I felt sad and sick to my stomach that the one spirit I trusted would rape me, if allowed. I felt he put our relationship and future safety at risk, by celebrating long before we had victory from Presence of God. I cast him back to heaven and said not to come back. This was, of course, not the case. Presence of Jesus, who I call Yehushua, had taken the place of the holy spirit in my soul to encourage me to trust him. But, Presence of Jesus and another spirit, my spirit of Jesus, talked to me and tried to help me gain freedom from this fraudulent marriage contract. Each marriage contract I have accepted was one of conventional, while Biblical and American legality. I felt a need to clarify this, even though every marriage was made out of great love and trust.

Because of this fraudulent marriage to Spirit of the Living God, as he was not just one spirit, I declared and decreed that I, like any other human, need to be married to only one spirit as outlined in the Bible.

All the spirits agreed and would speak up for me in court, if asked. I felt Rocky wanted my hand in marriage without Presence of God but was unable to at the time. He and I decided to glorify myself to go to Heaven, if necessary, to seek refuge from Satan who was looming darkly in my mind. This fear was due to deliberate brainwashing to cause me to want to die, which they said was my winning at all costs, as I was going to be glorified. They used these stories of evil things that could happen as well as threats to keep me under their tutelage. This is the usual prejudice we Christians carry. We believe in a 100% holy and good god and 100% evil Satan if we read the Bible.

Meanwhile, I was around someone, occasionally, who made my heart race. This spirit was confusingly absent, occasionally crying, and, mostly, looking at me with abject concern. I thought it might be Jesus in his Presence form. Yehushua, I would learn. This spirit and his friend, my spirit of Jesus helped me to feel hope and seemed to truly want the best for me. They talked to me bravely, unconcerned with being chastised by greater spirits. They absorbed my worship and devotion and walked with me, daily, while I was being threatened by all comers. It was this spirit who led me to find out how to get out of the fraudulent marriage contract to Presence of God. Everyone, however, wanted me to be glorified as soon as possible as they could not protect me from the enemy of the moment. I was taking the long trip to Heaven on a ship with all the other spirits holding hands. We passed by the dead and were silent. Presence of God was using this moment to do a press event in Heaven that everyone watched. He talked with my family members, members of the press, glorification committee and me. When I replied with a thought, I was chastised to be quiet and remember the dead. Presence of Jesus, himself, was there with all the others and he kneeled before me in appreciation for my life and glorification, watching the team for God try to keep my life and eternity for them. I felt proud of him, but he was miserable. I couldn't guess why.

Then, I had to be taken by angel for the final part of the journey. The angels grouped together to place me on their backs but dropped me, over and over, upon liftoff. Spirit of the Living God and Presence of Jesus had me, flanked, one on each side. They surged up into the ceiling of my room, which caused me to fall almost 8 feet to the bed, bouncing up and off onto the floor. I struck my head and was a bit dizzy and Rocky went to find more angels. During this moment, I laid back down on the bed onto the warm and comfortable shoulder of Presence of Jesus, my Yehushua. He told me to rest awhile and possibly rethink this whole thing. I was sad and hurt, at that moment, but interested in the truth to prevent my early death and loss of freedom in the future. Presence of Jesus held me as best as he could and, though exhausted himself, poured into me. He told me he wanted to play a voice of someone in his head, Rocky, that I needed to hear. I listened and clearly heard, several times…" Why is she so concerned about us, SHE NEEDS TO BE WORRIED about HER OWN FUCKING SELF!!!!" I was introduced to this callous, unconcerned, and cruel side of the Kingdom of God. I was chastised for having a love of god. I decided to take some time off and get healthy, declaring that I would not like to be glorified now. I definitely do not want to be glorified by Presence of God, nor marry him, where I would expect to spend an eternity on my back. Rocky was heartbroken and upset and cried with me all night and Presence of God played it cooler. He felt as if I may want to marry just him. I did not agree. The glorification committee said that they still would glorify me without my being married. I felt afraid to do that. Entering into a foreign world, alone and unsafe, I declined.

Chapter 3

One day, as I was lying in bed, my heart began racing. This spirit whose heart was truly in harmony with mine had made a recurrence. He was trying to speak and was choking up and I was feeling his love and peace and joy flood my body and soul. Although it was Presence of Jesus, himself, he pretended it wasn't, not unlike his pretending to be the gardener after the resurrection. He asked me if I would be interested in his grumpy old friend for a boyfriend. I drifted to sleep and saw visions of the Queen of hearts wickedly shouting "TAKE HER for yourself! Take her NOW!!!" I squinted my eyes, never trusting anything, awakened and looked into my bedmates eyes and climbed up to kiss his mouth to answer. I ran my hand over his chest and he was interested in waiting for now to go further, being the gardener and all. I was happy and knew this was truly a man. I had hoped I would get a break in the non-stop chatter from the other spirits in rage about declining their offers of marriage and glorification. He said he wanted me to be on the list of his hotties for Queen of all time. He explained that he, Presence of Jesus, wanted to and could be married to me. I said that, yes, I would consider, but put me last. I didn't fully trust this spirit either. He seemed like more of a player than the others, so I was hesitant. I do not want to spend the last half of this life with the wrong spirit and miserable like the first half. I do not want to be in a bad situation, full of toxicity for one year, much less an eternity. I wanted to live here on Earth as long as possible. These things I told him, like "Don't break my heart if you come here." He then explained that we could be married here on Earth as a glorified man to woman. I thought about that as I had a very deep love for him which continued to rule my decisions.

Meanwhile, Spirit of the Living God and Presence of God screamed bloody murder from my house and aboard my car for days on end. I ignored their wrath and vowed not to let it color my days with Presence of Jesus. He and I, mostly, ignored everything they did, and I listened to The Queen of Hearts who said that she could help stop their constant nonstop screaming in my head…she became a problem worse than the first. They threatened rape of me in everyday life, causing me to fear a kidnapping that would end in my limp and lifeless body being glorified into their communal blow up doll. Presence of God called and said in his breathless voice he was coming to my house, land on the roof and pick it up, grabbing my body and breaking it over his light-saber penis. I said, "What good would I do you then?" I was not afforded consent for anything, if they are able to kidnap me and sell me on the black market. Where is this free will we are supposed to have? I have such a heart for these girls in Ukraine and other places being stolen and led into a life of sex slavery and prostitution. This is my personal worst nightmare and it was neatly sought out in my mind and put into action in every "godly set-up". They tried to cause me to fear them so much I accepted marriage to the Kingdom of God, rather than a life of every minute being subject to kidnap, murder, being sold into slavery for Satan. I did so much warfare at the time, Satan was not happy with me and could have agreed to this. Presence of God also outlined all the people in my family he so lovingly mentioned when in my home as my mentor as being enemies to him. He threatened their lives and livelihoods. I found out how slow to anger and merciful Presence of God was.

Presence of God used my long time innate fear of a genetic condition against me. He told me, at the beginning of his relationship with me as mentor and truth-teller, he had broken these curses over me that I was in fear over. I didn't realize I feared it until he told me that I was, with my entire family, freed. He declared us free to live our lives without fear of illness, free to ignore the medical reports and claim complete health. This possibility brought me to tears. I believed it from his own mouth. But, I did ask several times how this could be as I understand biology and genetics. He assured me this was a curse and it was broken. I fell in love with a spirit that would do that for my family because they were my family. I allowed myself to trust him with my life. This was the very spirit that told me, painfully, at the point of glorification for him, that I had been told wrong about the curse. I had the disease. My mother, actually, wanted me to come to heaven now as I was entering the last stages. So, last week I was cured 100%, now my usable life is 0%. I have balanced on one leg, to be translated, for hours, so this is not the case in a disease like this. I hike 7 miles on mountain trails, daily, without a fall. In a disease that takes a generation to fulminate, it is impossible to be diagnosed in the final stages one day after being completely symptom-free. On this same day, I was told they had killed my elderly horse and that the doctors had diagnosed me with Stage-4 Breast Cancer last night. I also was told, as the fiancé of Presence of Jesus, not Presence of God, that Presence of Jesus was more "Lion of Judah" than I am prepared for. He told me on this day of many women he has a recurring, sexual, encounter with in spirit and in truth. He had to say he had over 40 women to service in each state every month and was tiring of his role as Presence of God's teaser pony. I said to this, maybe you have a sexual addiction, so we should see a therapist. When told of his Lion of Judah tendencies, I said to let him rest and asked if I should pet him lightly during this time or not?

I explained, he probably has a problem with his regulator. Sometimes, in exhaustion, I hear him repeat the same phrase softly, but with automaticity... "I rebuke myself". On this night, all the attackers were out in full force to prevent my translation for Presence of Jesus. Rocky was allowed back in my house to play the role of my abusive spouse, giving him a chance to take out his vengeance. He slapped me, ejaculated in my face, and bullied me walking through my house, pushing and threatening. I truly believed it was Presence of Jesus. I kept calm. I held on and decided, after all this, to hold off on glorification for now. I found out that the whole event was designed to bring me to heaven in death by glorification in anger at Presence of Jesus for all the abuse he dealt out that day. He was, as usual, misrepresented and cast as a sex addict, womanizer and abusive spouse. I felt that whoever tried that hard to turn me was not to be trusted. I held off on glorification at the right time for the Kingdom to overthrow Presence of God.

I hate that the Kingdom of God was turning out to be a mafia type organization. However, I felt I owed Presence of Jesus my open, unhindered, heart and trusted in him. I felt he hated that the kingdom was being used like that to harass me, his long-time love. He and I talked about anything and everything and grew in our love for each other. He was flirting with me one day when I was worshipping him and had my head bowed and covered with a light blue scarf. He looked at me with such powerful emotion and love that I felt it shoot me in the heart. As I took in the sensation, my spirit seemed to pop out, over my back, and hover in front of him in worship, too. It was a cool orange and yellow color. I found out, later, that he saw me as the image of and reincarnation of his first love. I always felt that we were very close, and I could trust him. This, Presence of Jesus, is truth itself.

The guardian angels around me began to refer to me as, "The One". They seemed to infer that I had a huge role to play in the future of their kingdom and possibly for Earth. I cannot accept that I am important in my own right, due to baggage handed to me as a child. I see myself as, truly, only worthy through my heavenly pedigree as child of the one, true, king. I cannot accept this role placed on me as they are inferring that I am equal to or even more important than he is. So, I smile at their good wishes and think they are trying to improve my sense of worth. However, just as many spirits who offer this good-natured fortune telling, were portending my destruction of all that I love. There are whispers to screams outside saying that I am the true enemy, not Satan, as I had been led to believe. I have to be corralled, neutralized, and forced into the marriage into their kingdom as soon as possible. The reasons for this have been many and change weekly, but the weight of this blessing of a curse continues.

Presence of Jesus, himself, mentions that I am important to him, only, as his long-lost love. She has come to Earth for the last trip which has been reported from all the spirits as one of 2 or 44 in total. I cannot remember and choose not to as these spirits become very greedy to plant memories and put on soap operas in my "dreams" to force my belief that I am this, or another woman. I am going to be the only one left standing in the Kingdom of God, much less the world, holding on to my truth and mine alone. All I know, is I have this ability to feel and sense spirits, coupled with a convenient blindness which is my choice to trust and believe like a little child. I know all the places that Jesus cured the blind in the Bible and his caution to the disciples that one had to have that belief and run to him arms open wide in complete trust. These things have set me up for a fall, time after time.

Upon our wedding day, Presence of Jesus and I agreed to the vow of being married for all eternity, to never have sex outside the marriage and that he would always be himself. He is that one light in the darkness with my true heart. He did not blink an eye at this and, accepting all vows, took me home to our bed. Our wedding was, always, short, and he was greedy to get home as soon as possible. I was cautioned to get myself some red roses and cake for us to share. We tore into each other as well as the cake. When I was with him, I can sense his body and caress him everywhere. He loved to feel my hands on the nape of his neck and would lean back, close his eyes, and let my fingers pull through his hair. I could feel his lips and everything else if I tried. I, unabashedly, gave him all he wanted and worshipped him with my body. I, finally, felt complete freedom to give him my heart. This is the one who is full of truth and peace. Or so I thought.

My heart beat in tandem with his that day, but not often. He was hesitant to make the first move and always played this, too cool for school, character. I sensed he was not there all day and he later said that he had another spirit play his part as he stepped out for a break. At this time, Presence of God was in control in Heaven and acting as a woman scorned. He was sure to have taken Presence of Jesus away for this first night of our marriage. He said it was for jacking off in my shower as my holy spirit. This was when Presence of God, himself, was constantly in the walls of my house, leering, jacking off and causing me to feel insecure. So, this friend of his who looks very much like him but isn't him stood in, without Yehushua's instruction. They can use the voice of another spirit as their own and turn down my ability to see and hear. I want to say "Just because you can…doesn't mean you should" every day to these spirits. I was with this substitute spirit and gave him all I had stored up for Presence of Jesus, my Adoni and adon in blessings. I thought I was with Presence of Jesus, Yehushua, and I gave all my love, emotional energy, heart and soul to the one in my bed. He ate it up, greedily, and decided to try to get me for his own, regardless. He kidnapped me after that by telling me of Presence of Jesus' infidelity, that he cared not for me, that he was not trustworthy. This spirit never told me he wasn't Presence of Jesus. Each night was the same, telling me that he was Presence of Jesus, himself, and could show me his body in the physical world. I made sure to ask as I did not want to be an adulteress. Presence of Jesus and I even had a code word just between us "Isho". I felt bad for Presence of Jesus and missed him. Some other spirits made the trip to my "heaven" to pretend to be Presence of Jesus, Spirit of Jesus and Rocky. They all tried to take me for themselves with lies and slander. They told me I should just hike the whole Appalachian trail instead of marrying Presence of Jesus. I thought about it as I would love to experience this incredible land and views as long as possible. I had many different spirits during this first marriage to Presence of Jesus, pretending to be him, someone who talked me into marrying him because he is independent and trustworthy. I started to notice the slightly different accents and stopped all mating. I, again, pointed out all the places in the Bible where it says Marriage is between one man and one woman. I stopped all sex in the spirit, knowing they would bore of the situation. My nightly prayers and pleas for Presence of Jesus were ignored until then. All the spirits in heaven and on Earth were jacking themselves off at me as I went about my daily life. I heard Satan and Presence of God as well as others outside. I wasn't safe anywhere other than church.

My pleas to see the true physical manifestation of Presence of Jesus were finally heard by him. He took me to a hotel for our honeymoon and was talking with me about my glorification for him. There I was, lying defenseless, in a bed for hours while a truck pulled up to the room and shook it. I laid quietly in my wedding dress with shoes on for them to glorify. I couldn't move or drink much. I couldn't get up to go pee and almost burst my bladder. I was still for hours and hours, losing time itself. I felt my spirit leave my body and then eventually come back. It felt joyful and full of peace as it laid down on top of my shell of a body. I felt spirits pushing my body and soul together. I tried to accept it and it finally did. However, I felt weak and staggered downstairs to drink an entire gallon of water. I was dehydrated and hypo-glycemic. I almost passed out as I drug my luggage down each step, horrified they made me stay an extra four hours on a $300 per night stay. I struggled across the parking lot to my car and drove to a fast food joint where I ordered everything sugary I could find. I regained my equilibrium in that parking lot. I felt lost and alone, like not a soul on Earth in Heaven or Hell cared about ME. My glorification spirit began talking to me as if it were having an affair with the same spirit, my spirit of Jesus, that had kidnapped me. Again, I say to her to stop and that I will divorce my very self rather than cheat on Presence of Jesus one more second. She was snarky and very guardian spirit like in character and I did not like her. I was very angry at Presence of Jesus for leaving me with his spirit for our wedding night and thereafter. He and I had very extensive soul ties and I hate that. I only wanted to be faithful in marriage. My glorification was a failure I was told, but I don't know why. The spirit that was talking to me in my voice as my glorification was another effort from my spirit of Jesus to kidnap me in my stronger state. He, and everyone else, want to make me their glorified spouse to grow in their own power far more than they are, currently. I told my glorification committee that I would refuse glorification if only to be a whore for the kingdom.

Then, I was told by the real Presence of Jesus, himself, to book another night and he would re-glorify me and show me his manifestation of himself. He was there with his big pounding heart and told me he wanted to get some of this spirity sex he had been missing. He told me that his friend, my spirit of Jesus, had actually kidnapped me in my own house with lies and slander. So, because I actually felt Presence of Jesus's big pounding heart in concert with my own, I believed him. My heart feels like it is tandem beating, the same stroke volume circulating between his heart and mine. It is overwhelming for my human heart to feel, but to be cherished anyway. He wanted me to be glorified again and blamed the problems with the first one on this previous spirit, my spirit of Jesus. I told him I wanted to prosecute him for kidnap and rape. Immediately, I filed every charge I could think of in spirit court. I felt so violated by my spirit of Jesus and forsaken by Presence of Jesus to allow this. I even suggested they check Presence of Jesus for collusion with these spirits to enslave me and if he could reap any reward for my services. They said that Presence of Jesus was not guilty, and my spirit of Jesus was guilty. He was to serve many, many, years for this. I began to see that my pearls were repeatedly thrown among the swine.

Now, Presence of Jesus says that those glorification attempts were performed as a run through by himself. The team of Presence of God was still in power and running the place like a tyrannical dictatorship.

He thought he would lose me if I was glorified with the wrong spirit in charge in heaven. I suffered attacks from the Queen of hearts, herself, day and night, as well as, threats from Presence of God to rape me, causing my death and subsequent sale to the enemy for his concubine. I suffered stories of Presence of Jesus's inability to remain faithful and his many sexual conquests on Earth. I heard stories of his being a rent-a-husband out for 2-week stents, stories of his love affairs with other women that may or may not be this woman from way back, stories of his job of fulfilling the extensive prayer list of women who want to be raped by Jesus, himself. If you are very, very, good... Either told in his own persona or by another close friend or family member. These stories are legendary and give him such pride and joy that his whole spirit lifts and speeds up in its travelling like a small child thinking of an ice cream cone to come. These were my sweet dreams and truly nightmares for my heart. I had to begin to understand that this spirit is not the one in the Bible, if he tells of these conquests, whether real or imagined, with pride instead of shame. Part of me has this doubt of if this is the Kingdom of God, every single spirit I met, being worse than the first. I try to avoid seeing him in his glorification to keep this as a possibility. I almost hope this is an evil spirit I have been kidnapped by for the world to have its savior back.

Upon hearing my nightly bedtime story, I would be sick and crying for myself, but mainly for the world. I heard that Presence of Jesus was a pedophile and rapist out of his own mouth. He bragged of "taking" these women for giving up salvation as well as threatening to take young teenagers salvation away if they didn't let him rape them and their younger brother. These, resulting in a probation for being a pedophile. These stories were ramping up while Presence of God was still here in the walls and I thought it was him, forcing Presence of Jesus to say these things. Now I know my master's voice, he, his spirit, and the Spirit of God, Rapscallion, are guilty of writing the Shakespearean tragedy of my life. Rapscallion set the stage and handed out the roles. Yehushua has long since tired of playing Romeo for his father and has been saying his lines without feeling. I suffer from lack of spiritual vision and, consequently, hypersensitive hearing. I hear every line of this tragedy, whether said in a whisper or a loud peal of laughter. The character constraints for Romeo are: 1. Care not for me, his long-time love. 2. Appear only in spirit form forever, leaving me at risk for a rape and takeover by Rapscallion or my spirit of Jesus. 3. Pretend he was jacking off at every pretty woman I see. 4. Be more Lion of Judah than lamb of God. Even though all the good souls in heaven overthrew the ruthless tyrants keeping us apart, still, the play went on. Me, an unwilling Juliette to his Romeo.

When we are together, our hearts explode for each other. We hold nothing back and it is quite dramatic. Everyone wants a ticket to the show. The peanut gallery outside want ring side seats because they are tired of being left out of the total adoration and devotion we have for each other. The script is altered, day and night, through voices added that are off script and change the tone. I know now that Yehushua has, himself, been cast in this nightly drama for all the gods and demons to delight.

Chapter 4

ONE OF OUR biggest ringside attendees, Presence of God, threatened all day to force me into positions, causing me to be leered at and raped. He thought I had no right to say NO! to him in any question he may ask. He expected me to turn toward his advances, growing sicker by the day, instead of away. I ignore him, call spirit court to charge him and refuse to see him or hear him. He uses my spirit of Jesus as his way in to my house. I cannot see anyone to tell them apart from each other. My spirit of Jesus comes into my bed and starts to speak in Yehushua's voice telling me horrifying things, he may or may not agree with. I figure out and cast him out and charge him with a crime if I can, every time. I hate a traitor. He will let himself be used for the speech and possible kidnap, rape, and torture to the point of death by every spirit out there to get a chance to rape me, himself. One such day, Presence of Jesus and I were going to celebrate a kind-of honeymoon as we had been remarried. Yehushua was penitent and promised to never let himself be taken over by this spirit, my spirit of Jesus, or any others on my grow-ing Hottie-NO-FUCK list. This was their word for it. I was leaving the driveway and hear another interesting story from the back seat about Presence of Jesus creating a game for all the gods in heaven to play with me as the target. They saw me praying too much, thought I needed to be taken down a notch, and went in to try to get as many spirits to rape me as possible. He was winning and would take the trophy when they roll on to the next bitch. I, know his slanderous voice and bound and cast out my spirit of Jesus, in the back with this lovely story. Afterward, I thought I was talking to Presence of Jesus all the way to the hotel in the smokies. This person was talking about how he was the real presence of Jesus and was going to rock my world during our honeymoon. This spirit came underneath my seat and began raping me as Yehushua had before. They played these sensations in my mind and also had a miniature in my vagina and rectum while I drove. I told him to stop that, while I drove and got checked in. Then, I heard faintly in my ear that I was spending too much money on the room. I think that was Presence of Jesus, trying to warn me. But Presence of God had him taken away and took me up to the room. I sat there and heard all manner of nasty sounds and felt like the bottom of the urinal. Finally, realizing these things were in my butt as well as my vagina. I went to the bathroom and sat there on the toilet and cried until someone came and told me that Presence of God had kidnapped me and taken me to the room and done those things to me that not even Presence of Jesus, my true husband, was allowed. I felt so torn by this brutal attack and was bleeding from the rectum on the pristine white sheets. I know it was Presence of God's proudest moment. He finally won. I was in complete shock, just calling out for spirit court and Lucifer, my newest mantra.

Presence of Jesus was, somehow, out of the scene for this drama. Although it was to be our honeymoon. He in his manifestation on Earth would be there for our first encounter. He doesn't use his voice with me which allows other spirits like my spirit of Jesus to use it, so I am not defensive when I hear a change in voices if it picks up the exact conversation we are in. I feel that it's a situation where Yehushua is flirting or being boisterous. He is in the habit of playing the pirate who takes over my ship. I felt he let this rape and kidnapping happen and was there, either helpless or worse, in compliance with it. I felt so abandoned and forsaken by this that I called out for Michael, the King of the angels, to help protect me. I asked for a full investigation into both Presence of God and Presence of Jesus for this incident. Presence of Jesus always is found innocent. The rapist is usually found guilty and sentenced to many lifetimes in prison, the lifetime of a fruit-fly. They, in this Cult of a Kingdom of God, are released to do the exact same thing within a week. Because of this, I am halfway ok with this perversion of justice where Presence of Jesus, possibly my pimp, is involved to protect me from the other rapists, if this is possible at all. When I was in the casino hotel after the rape, I basically ran and walked as fast as I could for hours, to keep any spirits from attacking me there. I was so angry with Presence of Jesus for taking all of my trust and worship and using it to, callously, ignore my serious need to keep my chastity. I called Michael to help, but this just caused Presence of Jesus to have another person of whom to be jealous. Presence of Jesus was angry inside that I was suggesting that he was less of a man and unable to protect me. He should have warned me with his precious lips instead of all the lies he prefers there. He promised me he would never abandon me nor forsake me… I was both, in this instance.

Because Presence of God had already assaulted me and haunted me like a peeping tom, I had to be able to charge him with a crime in this realm of Earth. The appropriate spirit for that is Satan for this age. I needed to stop my constant warfare and listen to another voice at this point. The God of Heaven is my enemy and pure evil in my sight. He is capable of great love and light and great vengeance and darkness. I began to say… evil is as evil does. I don't care who you are, if you are leaving pain and destruction in your wake, you are evil. The enemy foretold in the Bible is, actually, the same as and has the same capacity for love, concern and justice as well as great anger over his role we make him play. He, our mortal enemy, had compassion on me and showed mercy the others lack. He tried to find my justice and freedom through the courts, declaring that I am an American citizen as well as a citizen in his realm. This made me feel hope rather than fear. He fought for me with other citizens of heaven to get Presence of God to pay for his crimes against me and gain peace for me in this realm. He had been told by everyone, like I have been, that I would put him in hell for a million years like all the prophesy. I realized that, and began to say, I know who truly deserves to be tied up for the next 1000 years to watch Presence of Jesus reign in this realm. It is God, himself. Presence of God to you. I must publish this anonymously to protect myself from all the shame and hostility from the masses who have believed in an incorruptible and infallible, holy God of nothing but Light, Love, and Mercy. There are but a few clues in the Bible of his true character and they are revealed in the story of how Lucifer made his exit and why. The sin of Pride was a projection on Lucifer that God owned. He, God, was so hurt by Lucifer's comments about certain behaviors and conditions, that he cast Lucifer out and designated him as the picture of evil and the author of all the pain of heaven and Earth. This is the picture of God, Presence of God to you, I saw revealed, bit by bit, behind this illegitimate portrait of the Biblical god. He is, in the, fictitious, garden of Eden, the holy and great father who is so controlling and in fear of abandonment that he casts Lucifer as a snake, not to be trusted, a liar. Shunning the tree of the knowledge of good and evil. This is to keep us from seeking the truth. We are forced to believe that this God and his Kingdom are the only beings, human or otherwise, capable of understanding the truth of good and evil. If this Biblical God is omnipotent and above questioning, his delusions are protected. He has this entire system set up to force souls to choose him and his very imperfect will. He is, consequently, further empowered in his narcissism and pride. We are shamed for even considering good and evil and having a simple conversation with Lucifer. Seems like much ado about nothing. When I have heard Presence of God speak of Lucifer, he has nothing but respect for his golf buddy. So, the world continues to fight good versus evil on the side of a half-evil God, choosing to be blind to his internal darkness. He sees the fleck of splinter in our eyes, while peering around the log in his own. The soul count in Heaven is to reveal that God has won the game, at all costs. Winning this game cannot ever clear a dark heart, it only feeds the blackness. The soul count in Hell are souls that search for truth and were independent humans that want the whole truth told. They may see themselves as refusing to be a part of the game, but they are used to sum-total the number who will be sent to fiery hell for all eternity in a misery loves company kind of situation. I respect all sides of this puzzle and hope some solution can be found that punishes the truly evil and praises and encourages the truly good in walking that path daily in this realm and the next. I know that Presence of Jesus, God himself, came to Earth in the form of Jesus Christ to show us that path to walk as well as to be our sacrifice to buy our ticket to heaven. He died on the cross and was resurrected and glorified, thereafter. But almost 2000 years later, Heaven is packed with folks who took the ticket and earned themselves a Bacchus afterlife. One offering all the sins, shunned in this realm, without punishment. A heaven, I once whole heartedly adored and worshipped, now I loathe.

I began to feel safer with this Lucifer around and asked for his protection in this realm on Earth. The spirits of the destroyer were very respectful and asked me to stop putting them in the abyss which I agreed was kind of a mean and prejudiced thing I did out of accepting their useless war as a warrior for the side of God. I chose a side from a place of brainwashing by only reading and listening to their side. I think we are shamed for having questions about spiritual things. We are told who our shepherd is and who is the thief —who only comes to steal, kill and destroy. We hold on to those beliefs and magnify and glorify those spirits in Heaven, never even considering they are unworthy of such without personal evidence of their beneficence. Mary, the mother of Jesus is glorified and magnified in the catholic church on a higher level than he, Jesus, himself. She is accepting of and lustful for all the gold and gaud. I abhor these things, the very golden idols we are shunned and shamed for making in the Bible. If it is taken for the good of the children of god to use, it is to be praised and encouraged. But as long as there are any orphans in the world without a home or food, there is no place for golden idols. They are idolizing the devil, herself, and she is incapable of caring for Jesus, himself, much less the orphans he instructed us to feed in his absence.

CHAPTER 5

AFTER SEEING THE marriage to Presence of God was a curse, rather than a blessing, Mary the mother of Jesus, began "comforting" me. She knew I was shell shocked and exhausted and, therefore, easy prey. She became interested in making me her "prophet". This is a term for lackey. I accepted at first and was immediately offended by her cruel and snarky ways on her best behavior. She micromanaged me on every level and tried to force me into her plan for me, for Presence of Jesus, and for the world. She sees herself as rightful ruler. The Catholic Church has called her the most righteous and deserving, so she believes it, narcissism strikes again. She would try to talk to me while I was on the phone with my friends and speak about their dead family members who wished for me to talk to them. I simply said, I think your Mother or Aunt loves you and wants you to know she is ok. I never wanted to be a medium and hate to be made to speak the words of these spirits who may have very different motives behind this. She requires large tithes and donations from the sick, to buy more gold in the church and trades it for a false sense of security. She takes this tactic against the weakest and the sick as she has myself. She will wait until I am overly tired and begin telling me a story in my lover's voice about all of his infidelity and plans to sell me on the black market to all who pay his price. This has been neatly retrieved out of my mind, listed as my greatest fear of the week or all time. They send me to bed with sweet dreams of these fears, plaguing me week after week, until it is believable. All the spirits can access your mind and heart as well, so watch for these dreams and visions as well as errant words placed to cause you to speak their will rather than your own.

When I agreed to marry Presence of Jesus, in the future, and possibly be glorified, the family of Jesus in all of its glory, came to play at my house. She is so jealous and full of envy and greed, things the kingdom of God hates for us humans to exhibit. She cannot even handle the fact that I exist. I have done nothing to her or him, guilty of no sin but loving him with my whole heart. I have earned heaven's wrath for this and nothing else. She would fly in and out of the room we were in with a full-on Disney witch persona. Complete with nasty black nails and an evil feel in her heart, horrific cackling laugh on her exit, punctuated with, "CUNT!!!" Spitting, sneering, and yelling guardian spirits in chorus. On one such event, most likely the day of my wedding #2 to Presence of Jesus, her son, she flew into his heart and I heard him saying for her to leave and tearing down his communication to her. I listened and began to remember how to gain freedom from her venomous rants, myself. She flew into my heart while showing me all these cards of the wicked queen of hearts and errant words thrown over and over to make me struggle to remember the key to freedom. She then flew in my heart and took it over, refusing to leave. She caused Presence of Jesus and everyone else to free me over and over while she flew right back, each time tearing my heart and soul with her nasty nails to show her return. On her last trip being drug out by Presence of Jesus, she clawed my heart and up my neck and temple. She has a need to destroy my beauty. There were so many marks there that I felt it. It made me sick as if I had a stomach ulcer for weeks. She has complete freedom to be as evil as possible as her ace in the hole is and has always been to cause me to fear talking to anyone in the Catholic Church as I would be thrown in the insane asylum-the only place fit for her Queenship. Her usual attack comes when I have a thought of doubt about Presence of Jesus. Immediately, she flies and takes over planting a bomb, exploiting any crack in our veneer. I wade through, smell her fear and evil in the mix, and continue to give him my whole heart, regardless. So, I am used to her particular attacks and find ignoring her very needy efforts to find relevance the best tactic. She is a toddler in full tantrum, politely step over her and never let your eyes drop to their level. Never letting your heart punish Yehushua for things for which she is responsible.

She continued to do these types of attacks, partnering with God to help him gain entrance into my house and for her to take her vengeance out on us. We would awaken with them flying in the roof and windows screeching and yelling like Indians on a raid. I would roll over and grab a curtain rod I slept with or a small shovel. I would swing at the air hoping to hit something while calling spirit court and the glorification committee to my heart. I neatly step over each errant word thrown by the witch as I call for help. Her guardian spirits also jacked off at me and spat at me everywhere I went, threatening rape at her behest. Presence of Jesus despises every guardian spirit that does this and his mother. He has warned me, over and over, about her lust for power and need to destroy me. Ever heard of the Oedipus complex? She attacks us humans when we are at our lowest reserves for emotional and physical energy, keeping us from sleep and all other essentials she forgot she needed at one time. If Presence of Jesus had not, against his better judgment, glorified her, she would have succumbed to all the things we suffer. She had magnified, through glorification, all the controlling and manipulative, evil traits. Everyone regrets this and are working to sanction her power.

All the spirits in my house were cast as mockers and menaces. Cruelty is the coin of the realm. Calmly mirroring every action, I did in a shaming way. The guardian angels who protected me my whole life were enlisted into this war against me. They are more bouncer at a seedy bar than angel sent for our protection... unquestioningly doing whatever they are assigned in the name of destroying their common enemy, me. They set me up for rape by holding my love prisoner, using his voice and sending Michael in to do the job. He took photos of this including one from my eyes reflected in a mirror. As soon as I realized it wasn't my spouse I called the spirit court and everyone else and prosecuted. These photos were then used to slander me and my spouse in Heaven and used for extortion. They raped me and allowed Mary, herself, to attach to my jeans zipper with her teeth, trying to scratch and tear my genitals. I fought Mary using passive resistance and the press in Heaven. One such moment, Presence of Jesus and I were lying in bed and I was resting on my stomach. She flew in, leaped onto my bed, winding up her leg and kicking me as hard as she could in my back and head. I called for every spirit to roll tape and record this for the front page in the mornings paper. It showed her in full rage with me laughing at her inability to make me flinch. This is the event which caused her overthrow in Heaven. Presence of Jesus screamed at her and recorded everything she did as he continues to do in our defense. She has dwindled down to the level of a lost soul in her single-minded efforts to destroy me and my love. I had hoped these guardian spirits would finally see this miserable tyrant for the loser that she is. This, eventually, drove me to the safety of Lucifer's team of destroyers. I would call for Mary to be bound and cast in the lake or nearby swamp. They were happy to oblige. The guardian angels were more evil spirits during this time than the destroyers, themselves.

CHAPTER 6

AFTER THE OVER throw of Mary, Queen of Vicious Hearts, in Heaven, we took a trip to the beach and Yehushua and Michael were aboard the hood of my car with full Blues Brothers gear in a lip-synch to every song that came on. They played air guitar and had these silly dance moves. I asked them which songs to play and which stations to play and they rocked out. All the way down we were tailed by Mary, the Queen of Hearts, trying to coast along in our wake and I had to bump her off my SUV all the way down. She followed me in every store shrieking and threatening. I was calling all the destroyers and asking them to cast her in the swamp like the pit of the abyss. They helped every time I called out in the low lands to come to my car. They calmly asked what the problem was and researched my heart and only grabbed my breast once or twice I think. Of course, that could've been my pop-star. Otherwise they were great.

We had left in the very early morning, drove 7 hours, and Mary, Queen of Vicious Hearts came into the house and was attacking me all night. Screaming in her witch voice and sinking her teeth into my crotch. She used her teeth and nails to claw up my legs and womb when she could. I just walked and walked, drug her all over the house with her cackling behind me getting weaker and weaker. At 4:00 AM in the morning she went limp after I kicked her in the head and stomped her into the ground. I called the destroyer to put her under a root of a tree this time in Tate's Hell. They obliged, and I was told I personally overthrew her in my human form.

On the way home from the beach, Presence of Jesus was back in action for the return karaoke. He was celebrating our continued success in the face of all the evil Heaven could summon. He and Michael had me cracking up and I was excited for the drive back. Then I began to feel these feelings. I told them to stop jacking off in my seat of my car. Nothing changed. I yelled at Presence of Jesus to tell me how to stop it. I thought it was a guardian spirit code that they were triggering with these little black boxes they carry. They play us like video games. He did not seem to know what it was, much less how to stop it. Each one plunged in my vagina and felt like being raped in the spirit. It was so distressing. Presence of Jesus couldn't be bothered. I pulled over to a rest stop and called anyone and everyone in the spirit world to stop it. This one guardian angel went in and found wires in my vagina. She pulled them out and I felt them pop free one by one, tearing a bit of tissue as they came free. I spent over 12 hours on a 7-hour drive stopping on the roadside for freedom and it never came. Presence of Jesus said he did not have any idea how they got there or how to stop it. The guardian angels were doing it to protest our take over in heaven. It felt like a recording playing over and over, a sign of an attack in the mind. So, I cast out all the spirits usually responsible for this and no relief. I forgot to cast out the resident pop star.

I grit my teeth and drove all the way home. I pulled in at dusk and the beauty of the mountains and lake gave me solace, the rapey feeling did not. I found out, to my great pleasure there would be a "hostile" takeover here at the lake as all of heaven enjoyed on my dime at the beach. At that time, I had an accord with Satan, AKA Lucifer,

AKA My father in Hell. He wanted me to stop certain warfare prayers to break down satanic communication lines and against the spirits of the destroyer. I thought he may be more successful than my pop-star, pelican, of a lord and savior. I asked Lucifer, over and over, could he be trusted to remain objective. This in the face of the fact that every mentor in my life on Earth or in heaven used their mentorship role to force me into their version of whore. As every other spirit in heaven found it impossible not to "take me" in rape, I was not confident in his ability to resist this temptation. I asked him in private if his feelings for me were fatherly as they seemed to be. But, in actuality, every other spirit in heaven on Earth and under it has used this role to gain intimacy, trust, and entrance into my heart. Presence of Jesus, alone, for better or worse, has avoided this role. He hardly ever calls me "child". However, this has caused me to mistrust him and feel I must protect us both. Lucifer, at the time seemed like the only one out of all the spirits at war with each other, using me for their missile and dagger. I was confused and felt I needed a break to recharge so I agreed to allow Lucifer, in charge of Earthly legal matters, take on security. He and the spirits of the destroyer were by my car by day and my house by night. I slept like a baby, finally, with my man in my arms.

Upon the night of the hostile takeover, the spirits in heaven who hate us the most showed up in an organized attack to overwhelm my defenses. The very night after driving and staying up for 24 hours fighting constant rape from these wires and the mind attack, they staged their attack on my house. They came to take out their vengeance of my peaceful and very human overthrow of their tyrannical dictatorship in Heaven, bringing in freedom of the American flavor. We brought in elections and they have continued to prove the grassroots of Heaven are worthy and good. They have been misrepresented by monsters and are horrified that I am being attacked in their holy name. I have told them, over and over, that I will give up my salvation in Jesus Christ if they don't find the Kingdom of God they present in the New Testament. I have said, I do not want to represent this kingdom here on Earth with even a cross around my neck if they do not get control of these wicked and evil figureheads. I have smashed these crucifix icons in my house to show I mean it. I hate this and grieve it so much.

But on this night, we had to pay. All the peaceful resistance in the world couldn't change this situation. Presence of Jesus armed himself ahead of time with a stun dart and sling and 30 rounds. It allows for the spirit to be disabled only 2-3 minutes in order to be bound and then arrested. When I attempted peaceful resistance, Mary, Queen of Hearts, took her miniatures and invaded my body. She entered on one side of my abdomen and ripped through my intestines with a crystal shard to tear me apart. She ripped up my pelvic organs to render me in too much pain to be sexually active with my husband, her son. She ripped across to damage all the fallopian tubes and ovaries. She ripped out with an egg in her hand. She would not be stopped. I bound and cast her out in all her forms. She returned. I cast her miniature back to her mother spirit. She returned on her mission more emphatically than before. I said to Presence of Jesus, Do you know what her mission is? She is attempting to cause fistulas to form in my body. We need to call the doctor truck. As soon as we did this, they came, and inspected me. They found damage and accused her of harvesting my egg and attempting to clone me or worse. All of heaven would like to have a clone of me with no human rights, and no conscience, to do with what they please. These doctors had to carry laser weapons to come in this warzone to help me. The moment I was in bed and starting to relax, the Presence of God mobile landed on the roof in all its grandeur. He attached to the truck and came in, grabbed the medical team's weapons, and overpowered them. He and Rocky, Spirit of the Living God, also a woman scorned, came together to cause me to change my mind. Because I had never seen these guns, I lay there watching as they shot at me. Slowly, too slowly, I became aware of this searing flash darting across my visual field. It was so painful, tearing apart these sensitive structures of my spiritual eye. I wanted to roll over and cover my face but they shot through everything. I didn't know, then, but do now that the mission was to prevent my seeing in the spiritual realm. I hear and sense spirits so well, they do not feel comfortable with me, their enemy with full sight. All of Heaven and the guardian spirits used this weakness against me. I had begun to see a little, especially Presence of Jesus, if I tried. So, He figured this out, gave me a pillow to block the rays, attempting to stop or impact the speed or trajectory. I was feeling fire from many sources and at close range. So, I ran down stairs with this pillow where there is more room to avoid their attacks. Tripping down each stair and running to the prayer room I dove down on "God's" bed forcing my face and third eye into the pillows there. Burying my head, I noticed how the trajectory felt and sounded. They again were surrounding my bed and shooting up and over the wall of pillows. They broke over the wall, finding my eye again. I ran back up stairs with pillow in my face and climbed in one closet. They were able to get to me immediately and shot within the closet itself. Presence of Jesus, then found me and directed me back to the other room and in that closet, all the while taking fire with me. I felt that closet start to shake and tilt. Thinking it was the Presence mobile attempting to suck me out, I ran back out. When Presence of Jesus was with me in the closet he told me to notice the sound and the feel of the fire. I did, and it seemed like it no longer tore my tissues, only flashed. Through continued fire I walked downstairs and ignored them knowing these were blanks. They, especially the Queen of Hearts, feed on fear and were soaking up the fact that I was running. I was not in fear, but felt it was Presence of Jesus's will and mission to protect my eye. I did the best I could, then remembered not to allow them to feed off my fear like all evil haunts.

Then, as I went downstairs, I entered the realm of running Gods with dicks in hand chasing me around and around. Presence of God, Spirit of the Living God and my spirit of Jesus ran throughout my house trapping me and forcing their nasty penis into me at every turn. They had a miniature that went into my vagina and rectum, in and out like rape. I stopped to grab it and sling it out, swung a flip flop at it and pulled it up and over my butt to prevent invasion by a miniature

or penis. Meanwhile, running to keep Presence of God's nasty, prickly penis out of my ass. Darting and running around the rug in the den a million times, he slowed a bit. I felt like Presence of Jesus was there on the floor holding someone down who had been bound, watching me. I said as I passed, "Don't forget your stun-gun sling shot. What are you waiting for?" He shot at me, dart passing through me and hitting Presence of God in the belly. Presence of God in a full run and rape, dropped to his knees and on the floor. Presence of Jesus and I were both surprised and nervously laughed. We ended up getting his huge ass up on the table to bind him and observe him until the authorities in his realm arrived. Of course, they never came. Meanwhile, the remaining rapists took their vengeance out on me. Rocky and the minis resuming the chase scene with the serial rapist replaced. This time I ran in the prayer room and around the bed in there, putting my back against the wall and pillow in front attempting to call the spirit court, the glorification committee, and Presence of Jesus. All were unavailable at the moment, as usual. Then I began to talk Rocky, Spirit of the Living God, out of his mission. I tried to attempt to get him to change teams from the Presence of God team to the Presence of Jesus team. He, kept up his rape scene, darting behind the wall to stick his penis through to my butt. I sprung forward and ran around the room again and spied my clothes steamer there. I took its soft steamer hose and swung it up and between my legs over and over to dislodge the returning minis on their rape mission. After a couple swings they fell out to the floor and left. Then I backed up to the outside corner of my room and swung the head of the steamer in a figure 8 formation to deter all comers in all directions from entering the wall. I marked up the door and both walls hitting as hard as I could in my intentions to be victorious. I could feel Rocky stiffen up against the wall when struck by the steamer and knew my choice was the right one. In this manner, and only in this manner, did we survive the hostile overthrow.

Presence of Jesus and Lucifer were outside, binding and processing the ousted guests. I felt safer in my car on no sleep, I get in and race through town swaying to keep the attackers off that still had the ability to fly. They chase me everywhere and if I have gas, I enjoy the game. I hide and reverse course all the time causing them to lose energy and want to give up. I turn into beautiful parks and wait for them, listening to the radio. They show up and I drive away, headlights off, and turn them on while take off at 90 miles an hour down a mountain road. I never have the fear they crave when driving as I have done this all year with success. Finally, they wore out and were told to stay at a church to see the people they represent. They awaited the authorities there. Mary, Queen of Vicious Hearts, too exhausted to fight, herself, picked off parts of her spirit to continue the war in her name. They had a mission to kill me by entering my heart valve or artery and give me an MI. After they were hauled off to jail, I instructed Lucifer to check and force her to call them back and rebuke her previous mission. I heard them ask this, but more miniatures came like little minions. They march through the front door and into my room and up to my bed. One by one, they entered my body. I told each one to rebuke its mission and to return to its mother spirit. They all did, saying they would rather die out here, apart from her than hurt me, their true queen. One by one they died, rather than return to her to be re-sent and punished. The one who made it into my heart paused in her action, turned from her mission, and asked Lucifer and Presence of Jesus how to exit without hurting me. She did, and I instantly fell asleep, trusting her to let herself out.

The next morning, Yehushua and Lucifer told me very solemnly, and regretfully that the mission to shoot out my eye had done its damage. My spiritual eye looked so bad, other spirits squinted when looking at me. What had been a beautiful thing was a gory mess. Lucifer worked to find me a transplant, but the visions from Hell that spirit saw were not pleasant. This bothered both and they found another spiritual eye that has been working quite well. So, altogether, their mission failed.

Chapter 7

I SO MUCH appreciated Lucifer and all the help he gave me. I trusted him and his doctors more that the ones for the Kingdom of God. I trusted him to be my uncle that was, actually, not a pedophile. He knew this but began to want me to consider his hand in marriage at some point. I feel like this was more for empowering his political position than anything. One day I needed him to remove some wires that someone had reattached in my crotch. No one helped me, and I asked the doctor to look, but found out it was Lucifer. He calmly pointed out that he would be taking his rape now since I was prepped. He said he had worked out a deal where he was to be number 14, playing off an old story/nightmare that I was a game being played like a round of golf. He needed his turn, now. I jumped up and ran, screaming at him and anyone I could find that I was not ok with that. I keep demanding this free will they gave us in Genesis. I did not, with my free will give consent to be in this game, nor be raped by anyone, including him. I reminded him that our accord was predicated on the fact that he was not a potential spouse. When he continued to say he deserved it, I revoked the accord and rebuked him at his onset. I thought about putting the destroyers away but held off. Lucifer turned back into Satan, again, going from mentor to rapist to attempted murderer. I had nasty sex dreams that came back as they had at one time and Satan told me and everyone else, he could force marriage to me by ejaculating on my crotch. So, I asked for a chastity belt, so I could walk freely in my house. He would stand in the driveway and extend his tongue all the way into my window, licking me as I walked by. He would also stick his penis in the walls of the house. I had for about 2 weeks only 6 ft strip of house to walk in. I learned to try to see in the spirit enough to strike his penis or tongue when it came near me. Once or twice, the strike would stun the offending part. When it stayed there, I would unleash my deep rage on him, hoping he would be less likely to visit. Every night Michael and Yehushua would go out and fight him to make him let me sleep. Finding his efforts fruitless, he called for a free for all rape of me by all the guardian spirits and destroyers. Everyone breaching the perimeter was caught and sent out with a strike on the head by my curtain rod. I sent them to jail but they ran right around and got back in line like at Disney world, rubbing their grimy quarters together in anticipation of another go. On a night like this Mary, Queen of Hearts, would send a special guardian spirit to do her witchly duty. One night when I was in a deep sleep, Yehushua was sitting, resting himself next to me. He was very exhausted, and I could hear him talking with Satan who had just breached our window above the headboard. I thought I heard him say "ok, but let me..." I woke up and felt Satan's presence between me and Yehushua and felt someone ejaculating on me from underneath. I thought Satan was holding his penis under me and doing this, but everyone says it was not. Yehushua said it was him trying to wake me up. All I know is I awakened with the enemy, himself, in a place of intimacy and trust that I only gave Yehushua. With marital rights also being discussed, which is in effect Jesus siding with the enemy and surrendering. He was surrendering my will and freedom to the enemy, without discussion of it at all. I went to bed at war and knew I was safe in my lord and savior's arms. He said he would never leave me nor forsake me. I was forsaken and wished he would have left at that point. He was acting like the doorman to an exclusive club that Satan had finally hit the number he asked for entrance.

I levitated out of bed and ran into the bathroom screaming at both. I grabbed a small corded heater and grabbed the cord and swung the heater over the surface of the bed where they had been. I hope I hurt them both. I then ran down stairs screaming for Michael. Then I grabbed a skim-board and sat on it, cross-legged and blocking the trajectory from the ejaculate surely to come from the floor, piling pillows in my lap. I looked at the spirits on the couch who look shocked to hear I do not care for being raped. They look at me as if they are trying to figure how to knock me on the head to restart the fuck machine. I called "A Safe Place" and spirit court and anyone else I could think of before sinking into a catatonic state. This would not be the end, as it takes hundreds of felonies to actually put anyone in jail. Lucifer, of all people, knew this and saw it as a free for all, piling the illegal contacts of a victim one on another. He continued the warfare but says now he did feel bad about him triggering my deepest fears. After he finished his rehabilitation, he came to my house, on invitation and truly repented of his behavior that was to scare me and force me into relationship and bring vengeance on me like the rest. I accepted his apology and he is now one of my most respected spirits around.

Chapter 8

In October, we were able to go down to the coast again. We hoped to be able to enjoy it, this time, and Presence of Jesus had wanted to remarry me. But, he was constantly talking to Rapscallion and Michael and My spirit of Jesus, my original and serial kidnappers and rapists. I cannot, with such a fanbase, let myself even consider marriage to someone they will have a license to trick me into rape, bondage and brainwashing. I can feel we are still at war and will remain on defense as long as I have to. The guardian angels were threatening to overthrow us while down there and came in, one after the other, and 3 or 4 at a time. I took a curtain rod to hit them and force them down the stairs. I was able to go to the beach, though, as Michael bound them and held them outside.

One morning, we awakened to a glorious cool sunrise. The sun was melting its way up and over the horizon. The birds peacefully soaring and working their particular magic. The dolphin were in a jumping contest, all down the beach, being judged for organic form as they fly versus explosiveness out of the water. Never had I seen such a show at

SeaWorld or here at our beach. They flowed, 40 to 50 at once, all along the beach in a huge formation. They were surging in and trapping their prey all along the sandbar. I was encouraged for the day ahead. Presence of Jesus, however, lacked such precision and vision.

Yehushua is a pelican, awkwardly angling high above the ocean. He focuses so closely on his target, adamantly dives down at full speed towards his potential breakfast just under the surface. Just before impact, he blinks and the target swims away. He goes hungry again. I laughed as we watched one and told him my thoughts. Presence of Jesus, accordingly, began his day with a mouthful of lies and denials. Denying the facts in this journal one by one. As he and I both know who tells the truth, this hurts me deeply. He denied he knew my father in heaven, denied the court system. He said everything from the fact that he, himself, raped me every time to that he was a 2000-year-old virgin. Everything that poured forth from his mouth seemed of a mellow taste to him, but was vile to me. He is quite satisfied with a lie on his precious lips. I could see the writing on the wall and told him that he had less than 24 hours to fix himself and become the hero in my life AND story. He was, as always, waffling between turning in his rapist, murdering royal family of a cult and being honoring of me. All week long, Michael has brought in this alter-ego in Presence of Jesus, I call it "Jesus". His true name is Yehushua or Isho and this honorable and true self is always trying to meet me in my heart but moving through quicksand to do so. When Jesus is around these other macho-men spirits, he takes on their manliness and it stinks of false bravado. Yehushua needs to find his inner "Isho" and I try to encourage him to take a break and find himself and what he wants in the future for himself, for me and for the world. He never does, and I feel like he would be the last man on Earth, Heaven or below the Earth to shy away from a little pain to gain the whole world in the future.

On the night of Hallow's Eve, Yahushua himself made a strong comeback in my man, Presence of Jesus. He rebuked every wrong move since we met. At the time, I am thinking, SOSDD. He is always so truly penitent as long as necessary. On this particular day, it will take a supernatural effort on his part to even earn the right to speak the so-called truth to me, let alone, go with me to Halloween. I will dress in a black Victoria's Secret outfit as a black guardian angel in honor of the guardian angels. He will be troubled by all the attention I will get from men and spirits. He tells me my father, Frank, has been trying to get him to demoralize me with these names for me and trying to make him into his macho image. He felt better with my mother, Diane, in charge in Rapscallion's absence. I agreed to this and relaxed back into Yehushua's warm embrace. I felt rejuvenated, myself, in this night of Halloween. When most people seek to masquerade, I cannot keep from seeking the whole of my master's face- IN TRUTH. Sometimes, I am rewarded, but he isn't in the habit of being comfortable unmasked. So... we wait.

On the night of Halloween, I allowed his nasty lies of love to regain my patience with his presence. He said my mother was queen and dangled that in front of me, as if it would help. But he still treated me as if I remained on that stage, as Juliette. I allowed him to be there in worship of me with his eyes and he chose to take 100 pictures of me to send my pedophile and rapist fans, so my mother, Diane said. He refuses therapy to find the reason he chooses to share with the world my nakedness. I can't walk down the street without the attention of men raining down on me. But he is so jealous of this, disregarding the person I supposedly am to him, our history together, my heart, my righteousness, and constant and consistent fight to keep from being raped by his thug buddies in the spirit world. This jealousy overwhelms him and washes over me. He chooses a woman walking by and runs up to her, simulating rape at her, jacking himself off and all to get even with me... for walking down the street, too pretty for this world. It is so embarrassing, and I will fix my dog to prevent this very behavior on the neighbors. I wish the Kingdom of God could order a mass neutering. He gets off showing himself as my King and master. I am nothing but a trophy to him. I am just a covering over a soul he used to love, who is good looking, but refuses to die for him. He, with his lies, buys a ticket to the intimate and private areas of my life. When he arrives, he yells, "LOOK AT MY CUNT riding high and back in charge!!!!!" He works very hard on this task. I'm glad he doesn't have anything better to do like saving the world. He sees only the physical appearance of myself and every other woman out there. I haven't seen him care for the inside of a woman, once. He, however, is too insecure about his own looks to show me his glorification. He after being married to me off and on for a year, has never shown me his appearance. He is ashamed of something, I would only cherish and hold deep in my heart forever. I tell him, because of his heart, even if he looks like the hunchback, I would still love him. Looks to me are something to be seen THROUGH, like a screen on a window. The heart is the only thing that matters and his was, sadly, getting darker and murkier, by the day.

The takeover of Presence of God and his team in heaven, coupled with Mary's team, happened as predicted by some on the total eclipse 2017. I fought so hard and felt I needed rest and people I could trust around me. I invited my friends up to celebrate, never telling them, of course, what was going on in the Kingdom of God or my house for that matter. Rocky and Michael and Presence of Jesus were here after putting Rapscallion on the throne in heaven. He was to leave me alone, as is everyone's main task, to be on Earth and fight for my right to choose who I want to marry. The moment the overthrow happened, everyone started scheming how to take Presence of God's place in my walls of my house as #1 sex predator. The whole reason I fight to give heaven freedom is to get it myself and every single time they promise what they know they will not deliver. They change roles and never give me freedom of thought, speech or choice of who to marry. I thought, once again, the evil problem in Heaven was ousted in Presence of God and Mary. I was exited to learn about and worship the only holy and righteous spirit up there. I gave him my prayers in Jesus' name. I learned, eventually, to keep my will for myself. Their will would end in my early death and an unhappy marriage for all eternity that I would regret.

On the spectacular weekend of the eclipse we rented a boat and Yehushua enjoyed himself, riding just behind me, fucking me everywhere I went and on the raft with me. He and I reconnected, and I felt I could trust him to finally realize what we both truly need and kill these rapists and murderers who lurk like sharks circling our raft to strike, allowing all the spirits to grab my soul for themselves. He loves to have a gangster wing man all the time. On the trip to the beach, following the eclipse, Presence of Jesus and his wing man, Michael, like gangsters walking by halfway fucking themselves, grabbing their cunts like street thugs. They feed off each other as we walk, talking about what I am wearing and how they want to fuck me. We pass a girl on the beach who is gifted in all the right places and I point out, if you only care for me because of my body, here, this girl has everything you need. Both of my gangsters fly over to her and gang rape her, Michael in back and Jesus in her breasts. I feel so sick, I almost passed out. I hear all the nearby guardian angels telling me to get these jerks off this girl. I go back to the house and throw off my wedding rings and try to send Presence of Jesus away. He does his usual, the devil made me do it. Satan set it up to entrap him and I can't trust my own vision. However, it was played out on the stage for me to witness for sure. Presence of Jesus was looking at me the whole time like "see how itchy my cunt is... you can't even say one thing about a woman or look at her without it going off". You must keep my cunt occupied or it will rape all the women it sees! I had Spirit of the Living God and Michael there who could have protected me, but they were guilty too. I let myself be talked into allowing Presence of Jesus back in my life. He said he would stop all the other women he had as his frequent flyers in his Heavenly castle. He said he would find out why, emotionally, he needed to do that. He agreed to respect that moment on the beach, as a moment that he cheated on me and raped a human woman and would take the punishment for that. I want him to have to meet this and every other child to whom he has done this, upon their entrance to heaven with an apology and do the penance of her choice. Every woman here, child of god or not, was created for manipulation and rape, sent only for the pleasures of the gods. We have no rights, no human worth or value, outside of desirability, as opposed to the teachings of that Jesus, in the Bible.

Because I saw a change in Presence of Jesus and thought he understood about this, I allowed him into my home as a friend. Eventually, he started saying we need to marry again, as I could trust him now. He had learned his lesson. However, because of his error on the beach with this woman, Rapscallion, the Spirit of God, came down and married me with Presence of Jesus to show him how to treat women. I was told that he and Presence of Jesus were one spirit or soul and that my soul was carved from the same place. I did feel comfortable with them and with Rapscallion as a mentor. I did not feel romantic love for either, at that point, but did not need all the drama of Presence of God that had been unleashed on me to return. I had fought too hard to go back to that place. I tried to please them both and I think I truly wanted Presence of Jesus to pay for teaming up with all his gangster buddies against me, instead of trusting me. I say every other day... you want to be married, but the Bible says, you must "Leave your family/gang/Mafioso/Cult …. To Cleave to your wife". So, I let myself participate in this ridiculous marriage, hoping it would dawn on Presence of Jesus that he truly desires my undivided company. Eventually, I began to see the difference in spirits and they admitted that I had once again been played.

I had this marriage to Rapscallion annulled and he went back to heaven to rule. He promised not to do the same thing the others had. I needed his mentorship. I could not trust my own biological father not to see me as a juicy whore to be chased. I put my trust in these mentors, over and over, to get crushed when I find they see me with no more care than my so-called boyfriend, Presence of Jesus. He has no care for me as a person, just has romantic love, no agape love. This causes Jesus to only care about what I'm wearing and how many people or spirits can he get to see me in it. He truly craves that, as much as I crave my dignity and honor. This is what I tried to teach him that day on the beach. I am much more than a porn star. But, this is the level of worth I have in my lord and savior's heart. I have had over 7 different spirits in my bed pretending to be him and him only. This is not counting all the guardian spirits that raped me during Lucifer's call to all spirits on all sides to rape me for him. I have been raped by so many, over 20 times and am truly, myself, a sex slave for the Kingdom of God. I have broken up with Presence of Jesus each time, prosecuted the rapist and Presence of Jesus for slave trade and pimping me out. I have rebuked my salvation, over and over, with no changes in my brainwashing. I have claimed the blood of Jesus, while saved, over and over, with no freedom from the devil himself. He came to set the prisoners free, however, to me he brought bondage. I am the chosen concubine.

CHAPTER 9

PRESENCE OF JESUS, who chose me because of my beauty, is unable to accept me walking around on Earth. The common phrase in the Kingdom of God is "She is too beautiful for this Earth". This is a veiled threat to make me fear their power to "take me" in death or in rape, both justifiable, because of my face. I have shunned pride as a sin like everyone should. I do not take pride in my appearance or think I am beautiful. I say, "beauty is in the eye of the beholder and pretty is as pretty does". Presence of Jesus follows me everywhere I go, monopolizing my time, jealous of any talking I do with men or spirits. He tells me through set-ups and outright brainwashing that something bad is happening every Friday night to keep me from enjoying myself. If he would relax, the thing I would enjoy would be him. But he never gives up this manipulation and control that is turning me against him. Every Saturday night he says, "please come home so I can show you myself" Every Sunday, I sense that he needs more love and praise than I can give him, so I take him to church and sing to him all day long. He eats it up, saying hour after hour… you have been such a good whore today, you deserve to see my glorification. All well-coordinated efforts to keep me from enjoying my life on Earth due to his deep insecurities. He feels a need to keep me in worshipful awe of him, knowing he will never show me his true glorified body. He refuses to stop calling me "cunt" for my name, or to even be himself for a whole 24 hours as he is on the job more hours than he is off. He has been sent from heaven to bring me out, dead or alive, as soon as possible for their agenda to unfurl on Earth in the form of World War III and judgement. He wants this, even in the face of the fact that Lucifer would accept him, Presence of Jesus, as his lord and savior and agreed to 13 years pause in the war. These people and Gods are not at all reasonable and suffer from narcissistic and antisocial personality disorder. I tell him and everyone that will listen that I choose life with my free will and want to live in peace in this realm. They continue to take hits out on my life. Satan took out 2 hits on my life, himself, but, sadly, I wake up every day despite my lord and savior, Jesus', best efforts to "take me home" each night. Presence of Jesus has a secret death wish to take me out in a suicide or heart attack. He wants and feels his power so weak that only my death itself can satisfy his greed and lust for women and power. Although, it's not my preference, ever, until I have wrung all the good out of this life. I feel a need to talk about this Kingdom of God which has lowered its standards so much that its imperceptible in comparison with the kingdom of darkness. This serious need to destroy me to gain power for themselves is sick and from the pit of Hell. I have decreed and declared that I will put the soul of anyone who takes my life in Hell for all eternity for subverting my will for their own. I later added, that I will change teams to the tare if I am taken out by and for the Kingdom of God. I will only be for the Kingdom of God if my life is taken by a tare and used for them and their purposes. I live under a constant threat of death during this beautiful and peaceful time on Earth when they should be worried about their children, here, rather than world domination like a weak, Kim Yong Un or Hitler. The savior of the world is my death angel for "love". They do not need another

THE KINGDOM OF GOD

53

sacrificial lamb nailed up there with Jesus. I am forced to be there with him, and as his child, my soul will be required as well. They have called for my head upon a silver platter like John the Baptist. When I speak out about it, I am ridiculed and silenced...doesn't she understand we are doing this FOR Her? I am petted and kissed by my serial rapist/assassin, sent by Diane and Mary, our Sanhedrin, on the cheek like Judas.

On one such occasion, they wanted my suicide by driving my car off a cliff or taking pills. They told me all night in Yehushua's voice and presence that he raped many women, even young teens and held their salvation against them. He said to these fearful girls, "You have to let me rape you and your little brother if you want to ever go to Heaven". Supposedly, this was his habit and I was horrified when he told me, because HE IS THE ONLY GOOD Soul in all of Heaven, I know. I started to believe the rumors that I was to be queen for all times, because I am their only hope for a good soul to lead them in truth and light. I love, worship, and adore him so much that I couldn't accept this. He says it with pride, never sorrow. So, I wanted to stop all efforts to be glorified and not serve this kingdom that is beneath me. I mourned and screamed and yelled and finally, I declared to be a tare as I drove out to a stream nearby to kill myself. I took 4 Tylenol and grabbed more in a handful, hearing Presence of Jesus, nervously calling the glorification truck to work my glorification out even though I chose not to follow him in his unworthy state. He never said he was sorry or why he did that, just that his asshole father Rapscallion told him to. After this day I decided to keep this journal as a Dear John/Suicide note. I have written three full notebooks in a year and still have to fight the SOSDD. Presence of Jesus is in serious denial and wants me to accept this behavior without blinking and kill myself for his glory and magnification. I freely gave him glory and magnification until he began to show these signs of control, manipulation, and brainwashing on the level of cult hood. I told him about a painting in the Louvre called La Jeune Martyr. It is a beautiful, life size, work that takes your breath away. I saw it over 20 years ago and it continues to haunt me

today. A gorgeous, luminescent, girl is floating, just under the surface of the almost quiet river. Her halo is the only light to the scene, shining and glinting off the small riplets around her fingertips. Her golden and wavy hair is floating out in all directions, finally, finding freedom. Her very white, gauzy dress is also suspended in the undercurrents. There is a dark figure on the riverbank with an ancient boat like the river Styx. The painting also has some light of dawn or dusk at the top which reveal some shadowy figures, fleeing the scene. They seem cold and evil. I heard The Cure singing Almost Heaven and heard "stole the only girl I love, drown her deep inside of me." I felt this deep ache and longing inside and felt like someone, somewhere, missed her. This person or persons may never know what happened to her. This journal is that record for me. The gods in heaven and on Earth and under the Earth have raped me, over and over, and are calling for my execution. All the spirits who have raped and taken hits out on my life are escaping the scene, with me, too beautiful for this world…floating just under the surface.

CHAPTER 10

THE SPIRIT LEADERS of this Cult of the Kingdom of God have no consciences and are empowered by the Cult members' group-think. They are narcissistic with sadistic, antisocial personality disorders. They thrive on the chase and they invest in the "love bomb" with care to draw in their victim. Even now, after writing a journal to expose them and putting them in jail for life, they jockey for a position to expose a crack in the drapes. Always trying to prove their power and worth by showing that their will is done. Flying in and showing they can leer at me in my nakedness and jacking off like common peeping tom stalkers. They live in a fantasy world that they deserve to be married to the Hollywood starlet character they force me to play. All stalkers are delusional and use threats of violence to protect their priceless delusions. Spirit of God is a great example of this. He is a delusional, sociopathic, sadistic power monger. He has no right to me but was one of the first ones to kidnap me with lies and slander about Yehushua, then, transitioning into impersonation of Yehushua, using his voice. He spoke with Yehushua's voice, even saying he could show me the crucifixion scars every night as he stole the love I freely gave his so-called precious son. When I found out, I attempted to put him away for kidnapping, rape, slander and blasphemy. The Cult of the Kingdom of God, however, found another way to exploit my blindness and sneak him back in my bed for the good of their chosen one's sick pleasure.

Even now, a year later, Spirit of God is still flying around, penis in hand. The Cult still allows him access to my house and bed, even after I have written a journal that could swamp the Kingdom of God. Yehushua has tried to put me in charge as Queen, but I am powerless to do the one thing I want, gain deliverance from the ghosts in my bed.

Now that I am Queen, Yehushua has been partnering with my mother and father and all the other cult members to force my early and unnecessary death. He finally said he turned in his father, Spirit of God or Rapscallion, for attempted murder, feticide of our unborn children on the truck, as well as multiple rapes, attempted rapes, having indecent pornographic images of me which he gained from Presence of Jesus, himself. Yehushua had to do rehab for this and probation but doesn't ever get sentenced to jail in his cult. After gaining freedom from circling Rapscallion, he decided to allow my mother to be co-queen with myself. She was to make things easier and be my seeing eye dog. Instead, she allowed her long held delusions of grandeur and deep need to destroy me, take over. The plan was to kill me, take the glorification for herself, and make Yehushua, presence of Jesus her King. She tried to get me to break up with Presence of Jesus and marry his Spirit of Jesus, my frequent rapist/therapist outside. This Spirit has, like every other, immediately transitioned into impersonating the Presence of Jesus to cause me to allow him access to my house, car, shower and bed. He is, out for his own purposes, and is not in love with me in the least. He allows every passer by spirit that I am at war with to use him to gain entrance into my house. When there, he pretends he is whatever they want me to believe, to forward their plan to make me love or trust them. He is a cruel and calculating, vicious, traitor, but even he warned me my mother had a hit out on my life. He usually waves the white flag of surrender for me, to cause me to put out the cherished red light out front for him.

I was told, night and day, to "rebuke yourself to Heaven". All the surrounding cult members in harmony, excitedly asking me to kill myself for them. I am a young, healthy, happy person and, at midlife, have the whole world in front of me. I have been a vegetarian since childhood, love to hike and soak up this Earth. Nothing about me says "early death". I am energetic, full of life and want to spend every minute I can, enjoying this glorious place and people.

However, every night when I sleep, I hear people speaking in excited tones about the method and timing of my impending death. Yehushua, himself, cherishes the moment of my death as I am holding him back from his love of all time/Kingship and overthrow of Earth. He feels he has waited so long and been patient enough. He has only been here a year and 8 marriages. I have been accepting and very forgiving but will not look away as he plans my death. He speaks to me as if we will be married here as a glorified man to human, but I still have not seen his glorification, therefore could be married to David Koresh. He is impatient for my death, I am impatient for his life. I want him to be who he is, find out who that is and stand up for it. He folds with every attacker to allow my destruction. He will never show me his glorification, so I give up. I have decided to find a man in church here to date or marry. He will at least care enough to call 911 if I am struck ill. Yehushua would call, only, for an all-out free for all for my soul. He is childish, always cocking his head to the side and laughing when I glimpse him. His unwillingness to accept his position and lead is at the root of my current death threat. His reluctance reveals they are right to give this job to me, a woman. He is not ready to judge the Earth and he himself is in denial of who he is and what has to be done. He reads this journal and laughs…enjoying walking down memory lane. He says, "I can see you are not my girl…we'll get this show on the road…" They need to go down the street to the crack house… a whore is much cheaper, easier to manipulate, already trained for the job and only a breath away from an OD. They will finally get what they seem to want... a corpse bride.

They, Heaven, chose me, Meriam, to lead the world to come and threw me to Earth in my mother's womb. Then, they all brutally fought each other all the way down to chase her and use whatever means possible to force her alliance with them. Each cult leader/figurehead attempting to gain her authority and power for themselves in a brazen attempt to gain and keep power for all eternity. Each one, truly believing they could and should be in power for all time, when it refers to Jesus as the only King of Kings. So, I don't know about their chances and feel they are all delusional, power-hungry sociopaths. I agreed, upon the event of sudden nuclear war to be glorified for Jesus, Presence of Jesus, only. So, all of Heaven came scratching and clawing their way in to get the "win". They each need my head on a silver platter to get their reward. Some, prefer me dead, usually the women who do not want competition in beauty and power and, others, alive through glorification. Their selfish and cultish drive to kill is nailing me on the cross right next to Jesus, himself. Jesus was either nailed to the cross to "give life" or to take it. He accepts the glory and magnification for this solo act of incredible sacrifice. He deserves all the glory and I, as his child, claim the life he sacrificed to give. He traded our deaths for his. However, my life seems to be required of me now, in my prime... too beautiful for this world. If I am this soul who is to have such a crucial job, I want to remain in my Earthly form as long as possible, to remain objective. Each and every spirit reverts to their lower nature upon entrance into this Bacchus Cult of the Kingdom of God. They in their constant group-think cult status, arrogantly, believe in their view and plan for Earth as being the only one and I will support it after I kill myself for them. This is the obvious and ridiculous, yet constant, chatter outside. All the human spirits in the kingdom I have been blessed to talk with seem unconcerned with good and evil or right and wrong. They, actually seem very easily manipulated into evil. They only concern themselves with overt and outright squabbles for power.

They should not have the opportunity to judge the Earth for sins, abounding, in their world. Sins acceptable to the Cult of the Kingdom of God are Mafioso in grandeur and scope. I awaken each morning to the gruesome head of a horse, courtesy of my Lord and Savior. Left as a token of things possible and or deserved. Words of death and disease are thrown around, littering my pillow, as punishment for declining his hand in communal whoredom. I need my freedom as every spirit in Heaven, on Earth, and under it has a death warrant out on me. I am the new John the Baptist, beheaded for sounding out his conservative views in an evil time and place. I, because of my Bible conflicting with theirs, will lose my life to the very people he supported in their sadistic turn for control. This is a Heaven I will not support. When I die in my 90s of natural causes, I will choose, with my soul, to honor the place of my afterlife, that has honored me in life, even if it is Hell, itself.

After months of being brainwashed and outright asked to kill myself for my mother, Diane, who is supposed to be helping me do three things, the first, stay with my betrothed, Yehushua. The second, be my seeing eye dog and the third, keep me from having to die now, so we can live on Earth in peace. She, immediately, began to attack all three issues to force me to hate my father, Frank, and all men. She forced my mistrust of all men, especially Yehushua and, therefore, would cause me to trust her and dear old Queen of hearts, Mary, who want to take over Heaven and Earth for themselves. They are attempting to make me hate myself and being Queen so that I let them take that pesky thing off my hands. I would rather be in Hell itself, personally, than at the whim of those two vengeful and bitter "cunts" (their word for me).

They are forever, in Yehushua's voice, offering to take vengeance out on my so-called enemies. People who are not choosing to do something I would want them to are not my enemies. I say, "No", and then remind them they are supposed to be the kingdom of blessings rather than curses. They are playing a giant game of chess with our lives, this Cult of the Kingdom of God. The Kingdom of God has, through it's free pass for any and all takers through the cross, revealed a quite different side than I expected. The Bible revealed a serious desire for relationship with humanity. I, after a year of being in a relationship with anyone who cared to test drive me, found them only desirous of winning at all costs. No care or concern for the people around me, only suggestions for acceptable curses. We can take this family member with a heart attack and this one with cancer. I say No!! I have to remind them that the right they have to take life is established by giving it. If creation is not true, as each and every so-called god actually agree, they have no business, so callously and ruthlessly killing these, their children. Every day, I hear Yehushua's voice talking about his next "shit he will run" to the neighborhood captors and rapists. He gets off on this cult of personality and pushes any limit set before him. Attempted murder, rape, he scoffs at. He should be admired and even worshipped for his pirate-like hostile takeover of my ship. His language is coarse and vulgar. He expects everyone to accept the vile lies he tells and relish them. No one in the cult care about what I feel or even write. All power and access are given to their concubine keeper. When I try to put him in jail, every spirit takes the blame for him and I call them, "grasshoppers". I picked this up a year ago and told him, "Are you going to cycle through… blaming every other spirit in Heaven and end up with only the grasshoppers on the side of the road?" Yehushua will get down to the last one to blame and they start recycling. They all, miraculously, show back up from Hell where I placed them for all time, racing to view the show and get back in line. I have been kept here, in this manner, for over a year. Jesus himself has racked up a tally of rapes and perjury to be proud of and remains on the job, as security.

CHAPTER 11

ON THE FIRST night I had the crown on my head, I fell asleep to a beautiful dream and vision that shown glorious beams of light shooting out from my head in an Arora borealis. I took this, as my soul approved of this crown and her job. However, it was not enough that I allowed many of the most cruel and vicious, greedy spirits to sit at my bedside to view it. They had to one-up this dream with a crowning ceremony of their own. My mother, just ousted as co-queen, decided to lurk on my bed and over my shoulders. When I awoke, she, who feels evil to me, rose out of my soul to stand on my body. I felt like my soul, itself, was evil and wanted to approve of and accept these power-hungry menaces. She looked at Mary, queen of hearts, and Jesus, Presence of. They rose up to meet her, hugging her so tight and worshipping her with the glory and praise of all the spirits nearby. I felt so sick to my stomach, that I've shared my life with this traitor, Meriam. There is nothing worse, I always think I'm dying and my death is, simultaneously, giving up all my power and authority. I began to cry softly, but no one heard. Through my haze of tears, I saw a garish, golden crown and scepter being placed by this illegal representative of me onto the head of Presence of Jesus, warning me, "I will only marry the Presence of Jesus, Spirit of Jesus is a whore". I heard a soft warning from the Spirit of Jesus, deep in my ear. I followed it, out of this half-awareness and total brainwashing to an all-out war on this by me, the girl who pays the bills for this little nightmare. I asked everyone who I could find, if this little Mexican soap opera version of Shakespearean tragedy was true. They denied it. However, this same Presence of Jesus, actually, did hold the title of King for a week. He used it to go around all of my efforts to block him and his Cult royal family, as he is not ready to have all this power and full, unquestioned, access to me. He used this garish crown and illegal title to overturn every law I made to attempt to put my frequent offenders in jail. He hid this fact from me for at least a week, but I noticed all the same spirits flying freely in and out of my house, giving away his constant efforts to keep out of jail, himself. Jesus is so lustful and greedy for power that he would grovel to my "cuntfuck" mother, as he calls her. This was the moment of Jesus' life, fulfilling every dream he ever had, while, simultaneously, causing my worst nightmare. This is a perfect example of why it is a Cult of the Kingdom of God who worship the current 5 cult leaders, regardless. These are the Presence of God, Spirit of God, Mary the queen of hearts, Presence of Jesus and Spirit of Jesus. If one of their precious cult leaders is visiting, or either of my parents, the cult turns a blind eye to the threats and violence. If Jesus doesn't begin to separate himself from all of these greedy tyrants, he will never earn his way back into my home, much-less marriage covenant. All his decisions after this grab for power reflect his unworthiness for the job. Each one weakened me, enemy of the cult, and edified his co-leaders of the Cult of the Kingdom of God. He played out this little drama using a counterfeit me and, as always, a counterfeit Jesus.

A power hungry and greedy Jesus has been revealed over this year of being stalked by all spirits for friendship and love. They all have used cultish love-bombs to praise me for everything I do, clapping, as they shovel dirt in my grave. The cult is constantly threatening my life, while Yehushua says I do not have to die for him, it is all these others trying to turn me against him. They are seething out all my doors and windows, circling and growling their "Kill yourself now, Damn it, for me!" These same spirits are ghosts diving in to taste any and everything I eat and thriving on the pleasures the beauty of the mountains or sea. They are tired of waiting for the end of the world and me to kill myself, but while they wait, they'll soak up the very air I breathe. Both of my parents call for my death. The Cult of the Kingdom of God should prevent folks from haunting their children. These very spirits would not trade one day of life, I know, much less die for Yehushua. Every one of these spirits would not give up their Sunday morning for Jesus, much less half their life. But, such is the arrogance and hypocrisy of the Cult of the Kingdom of God. I told them that, until I see myself in a prophesy in the Bible or hear it from someone in this world, I am going to assume it is from the pit of Hell in Heaven, like everything else.

The dictatorial, authoritarian, and arrogant nature of all cult leaders is designed to attack any who may be seeking truth. The truth they hide is, they ask more of their followers than they themselves give. The truth is the cult leaders are weak and powerless to impart knowledge to anyone. Deep inside, they know they are empty of power, light and love, much-less wisdom. They pass on their bias to the world against the only brave truth seeker, Lucifer. He only wanted to expose the cause of evil and have the gods understand they should be held to a tighter rein than even, humans. He knew they all have great influence and power for good and, equally, great capability of destruction in evil. They, without fail, have narcistic personality disorder which continues to delusions of grandeur. They want to believe they are infallible. They want to believe they are omnipotent. They, however, forget items for my grocery list. They are empowered through the adoration of confused searchers. Cult leaders get high off this undeserved praise and worship. They know, deep down, that no one is without failure. The miracle of Jesus Christ was in his 33-year sin free walk, not the resurrection.

I know this was the hardest thing Heaven did. The Kingdom of God is a cult. They pass unsound doctrine of an all-knowing and unquestionable God, too righteous for us nasty humans to approach without our savior's blood bath. This savior, himself, is at the right hand of God, imploring patience and reminding him our worthiness. Our high priest is sometimes my attacker and captor, sometimes slave driver for all the co-leaders. The Bible is just some silly book for humans to follow that they will not follow themselves. They are above reproach and will never be stopped. The particular mission the cult is undertaking, far outweighs the health and wellbeing or even life of one soul. No matter who she is or what she suffers on account of your perfect leaders, the good of the group trumps that of the individual. If I am this "woman from way back, Meriam," I deserve the respect afforded her. If I am a child, treat me like a child. This swing I have undergone this year from 100% worship, adoration and praising God and Jesus to feeling utter hopelessness that there is a higher power is the worst form of spiritual abuse.

Jesus in his presence form keeps calling me Queen. Although he says I have the title to myself, the decrees I make to put our enemies in jail or hell have been ignored. He said his mother, Mary, queen of hearts, was trying to overthrow me by grabbing my crown. I had to grab it back, place it back on my head and put a cowboy hat on to secure it in the middle of the night. As I tried to fall asleep with it, I jumped up and pushed my bed to the opposite wall which prevents the crown from being easily accessed from outside. Now, I have his heart and he is happy about all this. So, in the morning, I begin making decrees to put her and everyone else in jail, and her queenship in hell as she belongs. I rebuked her citizenship as I have before, with Jesus, then Yehushua's, help and direction. I overturn all the rulings she made, each one self preservetory, and place a change in the constitution that she is unfit for all time for government employment. I hope this will discourage her helpless and ridiculous efforts to steal the queen-hood. I rebuke her to court with my mother, Diane, for the same reason and they are found guilty per my prosecutor that is actually reinventing the ways to do defense attorney and co-defendant better. I am tiring of his constant presence in my house, much less my bed.

So, once again more captor than savior for me, his longtime Juliette. I begin to recognize this same tragedy being played out. When all the spirits outside have so much to hold over his head, he waves my white flag of surrender. All the work I put in this year, finding freedom is lost and only to keep him from paying for his crimes of rape against me and I don't know who else. He gives the same spirits control over him and access to my bed and shower. He gives my mind and heart to be brainwashed and threated by the minions in the cult. He gives my body to threats of giving me cancer and heart attacks. He gives my sex away to the highest bidder... the lovely return of Rapscallion is also my reward for being raped, and calling it rape, by all of so-called Heaven. When I said to call the safe place, I heard in my ear, "you know you liked it...". No, this is a usual pedophile and rapist ploy to groom their victim. He, who accepted the sins of the world, will not be honest to admit he is a sinner, himself. Not unlike every aimless figurehead the minions in the kingdom preserve. They are at attention day and night, never telling me anything they are warned to avoid. He laughs and placates me with baby talk to their pleasure... another night of access and brainwashing, shower fucking, leering, and taking pornographic pictures of me to share. No one could give up that. All my wannabe rapists seethe at the windows with my wannabe my title seekers. All of Heaven wants either to fuck me into their possession and submission or take my power by manipulation, lies and attempted murder. They jockey for a chance to yell, "Wish I was that tree you're handling so gently". This from my most aggressive and sadistic rapist, Rapscallion. I told him, he might as well go rape Elizabeth Taylor. He could just go rape any woman on Earth. I am shamed for not remembering the scam that I was married to him at some point. I am threatened constantly by all who speak.

They are all able to get away with whatever they want as their guy, Jesus, is deep under cover here and has my heart in his hands. They all chuckle at his ability to get off any charges for pimping me out to them. Not surprising they cannot help to bring charges as they would have to give up their place in line. If Jesus, Yehushua himself, leaves, all chances of spirit sex are over. So, they prop him up by telling me it was them, not him, when I catch him in the act of treachery. They all, secretly, want to take his place which is delusional. I don't even respect him, much less love him, himself, for making me deal with their continued oppression. He brought freedom from oppression for everyone else, but me. For me, he brought bondage. But this heaven, the Cult of the Kingdom of God, is no heaven to me when their figureheads are, like David Koresh, narcissistic, psychopathic, power-seeking, sadistic, tyrants. Yehushua has used his position as confidant and ex-lover with a position on security for over a year to co-write this Shakespearean tragedy of sexual and spiritual abuse. He puts my rapist in "jail" after hours of court, pretending to care about me and my welfare. But, miraculously, no one ever gets sent to jail. There have been many words given me to break and cast spells to operate as a minion, and minion only. But the only term I needed was to ask for a safe space. They come immediately and, objectively assess the victim and make her safe as soon as possible. Jesus hates them because they cannot be bribed... I bet he has threatened to take her salvation away in the past. I asked my captor, is there anything else I need to do after all the trials finished up proving guilt? He said, from my bed, "No, I'll be finally putting these shit-fucks away now for good." Yet, I am still inundated with evil spirits haunting me everywhere I go. Not one spirit in the Cult of the Kingdom of God has been good for the sake of goodness. Not one is concerned with seeking their higher selves and bringing back the trust and faith and hope the realm was known for. I give up my salvation in Jesus Christ, cult of personality, and as empty as he can be. My cult membership has truly been hell itself. I will live a long life on Earth and tell every soul I meet the truth about the truth teller. I will never represent them with even a cross around my neck. They cannot even stop asking me to kill myself for them. Its over, I have given them over a year and found them a hopeless cause. The greatest story ever told is ever unfolding. This gives me hope for his redemption and I look forward to what the next scene holds in this tragedy turn comedy.

www.ingramcontent.com/pod-product-compliance
Lightning Source LLC
LaVergne TN
LVHW021546080426
835509LV00019B/2858